IGDRASIL.

IGDRASIL;

OR,

THE TREE OF EXISTENCE.

BY

JAMES CHALLEN,

AUTHOR OF THE CAVE OF MACHPELAH, AND OTHER POEMS.

PHILADELPHIA:
LINDSAY AND BLAKISTON.
1859.

STEREOTYPED BY L. JOHNSON & CO.
PHILADELPHIA.
C. SHERMAN & SON, PRINTERS.

I LIKE, too, that representation they have of the tree Igdrasil. All life is figured by them as a tree. Igdrasil—the Ash Tree of Existence—has its roots down in the kingdoms of Hela, or death: its trunk reaches up heaven-high, spreads its boughs over the whole universe: it is the tree of Existence. At the foot of it in the death-kingdom sit three Normas,—Fates,—the Past, Present, Future, watering its roots from the sacred well. Its boughs, with their buddings and disleafings,—events, things suffered, things done, catastrophes,—stretch through all lands and times. Is not every leaf of it a biography, every fibre there an act, a word? Its boughs are histories of nations. The rustle of it is the noise of human existence,—onwards from of old. It grows there, the breath of human passion rustling through it, or storm-tost, the storm-wind howling through it like the voice of all the gods. It is Igdrasil, the tree of Existence. It is the past, the present, and the future. What was done; what is doing; what will be done. The Infinite conjugation of the verb "TO DO."

CARLYLE.

PRELUDE.

Chorus.

I.

SILENCE.

I HAVE dwelt alone,
  Voiceless, breathless, still;
Not a sigh or groan
  The hungry air could fill.
Not a sound, a word,
  Falls upon my breast;
And Echo has not stirred
  The quiet of my rest;—

II.

NIGHT.

                    Not alone,
  For I ever with thee dwelt;
Round thee I have thrown
  My dark, mysterious belt:
Not a sound or sight,
  Not a gleam of fire,

Not a ray of light,
  My languid thoughts inspire.
O darkness, flee away,
  I perish with the cold.
Send me the light of day:
  I am growing old.

III.

SPACE.

Within my ample bound,
Ye two alone are found.
    We three;—
The offspring of Infinity.
With shuddering fear
I listening hear,
From out the deep profound,
The all-creating sound,
Which from the silence breaks;
And the loud "Let there be," my spirit
    shakes.
And from the hungry night,
Lo! now is born the Light;
And in my arms I fold,
And will forever hold,
All things, which from the Infinite hath
    rolled.

LIGHT.

Forth from the light a spirit came,
  Robed with a scarf of dazzling hue;
He seemed, at first, a radiant flame,
  Breaking from out the distant blue.

Farther than sense or thought can fly,
  In depths untrodden, was he seen,
Beyond the trooping stars on high,
  Or where they send their arrows keen.

The virgin light around him flung
  All colors, which are seen at even;
Or which the morn has ever hung
  Upon the opening gates of heaven.

Graceful as matin rays of light
  That float upon the ocean's wave,—
He burst upon the enraptured sight,
  Within the luminous floods to lave.

Silence was startled with his wings,
  That fanned the sleeping breath of song;
And o'er the realms of Night he flings
  His golden arrows, swift and strong.

And SPACE now filled his ample bound
With suns and systems, worlds of fire,
Which since have run their restless round,
And never shall in death expire.

And as he flew from star to star,
And lit their lamps with golden light,
He sought our gem-like orb afar,
And found it in his onward flight;—

So distant from the realms of morn,
Which gave erewhile his glorious birth,
No ray of light, as yet, was born
Upon our lone and slumberous earth.

He spread his radiant scarf upon
Her form, so beautiful and bright;
And as her face with glory shone,
He left her, half in shade and light!

'Twas not by chance, but by design,—
Prophetic of our future race,—
The meaning of that ominous line,
Which time nor distance can efface.

Sleep and unrest, the shade and light,
Contending still! nor shall the day

Conquer the ancient realms of night
  Till brighter suns their powers display.

When quick, as from the orient leaps,
  The quivering beams of rising morn
From hill to hill;—till onward sweeps
  The sun's broad light, on pinions borne;

So came there myriad spirits blest,
  Filling the mighty void afar,
Each bearing on his blazoned breast
  A glowing, bright, and burnished star.

All orbs that deck the milky way,
  Or blaze around the Arctic seas;
Or those that chaunt their solemn lay
  Near to the Southern Cross,—to these

Were as the drops of morning dew
  That sparkle o'er a heath-grown field,
To the broad ocean's ample view,
  Should he his watery treasures yield.

And as the earth, in form so fair,
  Rose from her ancient womb of night;
She robed herself in garments rare;—
  A queen among the Peers of light.

And deep within her heart there lay
  A precious seed,—divine its birth;
Ready its glories to display
  Upon the waiting, anxious earth.

And, as it broke beneath the mold,
  At once it grew in air and grace;
The richest treasure earth can hold,
  Divine in presence, form, and face.

And as it waved its branches high,
  And all its blooming beauties spread,
A warder from the distant sky
  Its future history sung or said.

IGDRASIL.

PART FIRST.

THE ANGEL'S SONG.

A WONDERFUL tree is the tree Igdrasil!
Through all ages it grew, and it grows ever still;
In the kingdoms of Hela far down are its roots,
And as wide as creation it sends forth its shoots—
This tree Igdrasil!

At its foot sit the Normas, the house where
they dwell,
To water its roots from their deep sacred
well;
The past and the present, the future, are there,
In union their labors incessant to share,
On this tree Igdrasil.

It has seen kingdoms rise, it has seen them
decay,
It has lived through the past, it will live on
through aye;
'Neath its shade have all nations, all peoples,
been found,
And its leaves and its fruitage are scattered
around,
Of this tree Igdrasil.

Its boughs stretch now earthward, now heaven-
ward, far
As the line of existence, the light of a star;

Through all seasons, all ages, all changes of
time,
It grows, buds, and blossoms, in every clime,
This tree Igdrasil.

The buds still are swelling; its blossoms appear
Every moment and hour, every day in the year;
And a dower of wealth, on the earth, on the
main,
It as constantly sheds, thick as dew or the rain,
From this tree Igdrasil.

The wind from all quarters is shaking its
leaves;
And, sweeping its branches, it solemnly weaves
Misereres, cantatas, old chorals and songs,
And its grand Oratorio all nature prolongs,
Of this tree Igdrasil.

Even now, mid the leaves of this far-spreading
tree
May be heard the loud sobs of its sad litany,

Which the children of sorrow pour forth on
the gale,
As the murmuring wind bears along the wild
wail
Through this tree Igdrasil.

In the fresh bloom of morning, at noon, and
at night,
Mid the shadows of even, the glare of the
light,
Now slow onward moving, now swift as the fire
From the dark thunder-cloud, is the sweep of
its lyre
Through this old Igdrasil.

Mid earthquake and tempest, through flood
and through fire,
Its branches are climbing yet higher and higher;
And its shadow still deeper and deeper is
grown:
Of this world the sole tenant, it stands all alone,
This brave Igdrasil.

The cedars of Lebanon fall one by one;
The oaks of old Bashan lie dead as a stone;
The pride of the forest, the king of each
hill,
Fall to dust when the mission of life they
fulfil;
But not so Igdrasil.

Green and golden, the light through its verdure
now streams,
And like arrows are flying the swift-glancing
beams
On the hill-tops and meadows, on rivers and
lakes,
And the bird of the wild woods the rapture
partakes
Of this old Igdrasil.

Gentle May, mid the blossoms that fall from its
crown,
Fills her bosom with flowers, and aweary sits
down

To entwine them in wreaths, of all colors and hues,
In the freshness of morning,—its sunlight and dews,
From this tree Igdrasil.

And Summer, with lap and with bosom replete,
And wading through oceans of bloom 'neath her feet,
Exhausted and faint, has now fallen asleep;
While the birds in the branches a festival keep
In the old Igdrasil.

And Autumn then comes, in the wane of the year,
When the fruits are all ripe and the leaves crisp and sear;
And to gather the harvest, a strong thrifty swain
To work he now summons his bold, rustic train
Round the old Igdrasil.

The baskets are bursting, and in heaps all
around,
Thick as hail, the rich fruitage is seen on the
ground;
And the large, ponderous wain with its burden
now groans
And its wheels harshly creak as they grind o'er
the stones
'Neath the old Igdrasil.

Stern Winter gives warning that now he is near,
And he sends a sharp whistle, coldly keen, and
most clear;
And he claims all the flowers of Summer and
Spring,
And the fruits of the Autumn,—the covetous
thing!
Of this rich Igdrasil.

On its head all the day is the sun shining bright,
And a crown of rich gems shed their radiance
at night;

But the brightest of things shows a shadow as
dense,
Like the sun when its disc is concealed from
the sense:
So this tree Igdrasil.

Sin and shame, guilt and sorrow, have furnished
the braid
Which has woven the deepest, the deadliest
shade,
Underlying the arms and the leaves of this tree;
In the churchyard and lone grave their work
you may see,
'Neath the old Igdrasil.

Smiling infancy there, with old age now abreast,
And manhood and youth, all are taking their rest;
One by one, chosen quick, or by strong currents
swept,
Here they lie side by side,—both the hated, the
wept,
'Neath the old Igdrasil.

O tree, noble tree, with thy roots deep and
 strong,
Sending forth thy rich sap to each outermost
 prong,
With thy trunk knit and twisted, more solid
 than steel,
Yet with fibres which keenly, most vividly,
 feel!
 Grow on, generous tree!

Still add to thy girth new accretions and bands,
Spread out till thy bounds shall encompass all
 lands;
Shed thy rinds scathed and blighted, and hoary
 and sear,
To enrich and to fatten thy soil every year,
 O huge mountain tree!

Reach forth thy brave arms, brawny, massive,
 and sound,
Till their shadows shall cover earth's uttermost
 bound,

And their fruitage and leafage shall ripen and
wave
In all lands and all zones, both to comfort and
save,
O giant-like tree!

From thy branches a shoot has sprung up to
the skies,
And its fruit is more rich than has ere blessed
our eyes;
It has caught all the dews and the sunshine
of heaven,
And a dower on thy head now most richly is
given,
O loved, honored tree!

It is sending thy juices in health back again,
Distilling its sweets, like the God-gifted rain,
On the heath-flowers, and pansies, and roses that
bloom
In the hot parchéd deserts and mouldering tomb,
O heaven-blessed tree!

It is bending its branches and crowning thy
head,
With a scarf bright and beautiful over thee
spread;
Its leaves never wither, its flowers ne'er decay,
And its fruit, hence immortal, shall ne'er fall
away,
O grand, kingly tree!

Soft and silken its tendrils; in velvety down,
Trailed and plaited, they hang from thy rich
amber crown,
Of all colors that hide mid the flower-covered
leas,
Or the breeze-scented mountains, the mirroring
seas,
O rich, braided tree!

In its o'erbending boughs, gently waving on
high,
Precious fruits are seen ripening beneath the
warm sky;

And ethereal dews all the night freshly shed
Their odorous sweets on its garlanded head,
O light-loving tree!

Soft murmurs, faint breathings, Æolian and sweet,
Silver-toned and euphonious, in their rhythmical beat
Now chime with the voices of angels, which swell
The rich music that breaks over mountain and dell,
O song-loving tree!

Dissolving like dew on the low creeping grass,
When the sighs of the heart-broken upwards do pass;
Or like thunder that breaks o'er the dark, troubled wave
When the hopes of the free are struck down to the grave,
O merciful tree!

When the tears of the penitent fall on the
earth,
Their soft cadence awakens thy rapturous
mirth;
And when infancy sends forth its last pulsing
wail,
Invisible strings melt in gladness the tale,
O deep-troubled tree!

When grief sits alone, clasping firmly each
palm,
It is thine to allay all its sorrows with balm;
And when sadness sits brooding o'er anguish
and care,
Thou canst change by a touch all its sighs into
prayer,
O pitying tree!

Or when sleep flies the eyelids or dreams mock
the rest,
Morphean founts are awakened and pour from
thy breast;

And when, fainting and weary, they sink in
despair,
Fragrant scents, as of violets, breathe through
the air,
O grief-drowning tree!

And when hosts gather round us to smite down
the free,
"The sound of a going" is heard on this tree;
'Tis the star-trooping angels that sweep through
the sky,
To rouse us to battle and aid us on high,
O truth-loving tree!

O rich fragrant tree! O flowering tree!
In the shades of thy bowers I sit musingly;
And I hear dulcet chimes, like the low, tinkling
sound,
Born of silence, that breathes from the moss-
covered ground,
O myriad-voiced tree!

PART SECOND.

I.

In times of old, mid shadows dim,
Pale forms were seen, both blithe and grim;
Here Proserpine affrighted stood,
Or gliding through the sheltering wood;
And sylvan nymphs, and even old Pan,
Scattered flowers as they ran.
And, as in cathedrals gray,
Where the nuns their vigils pay,
Or the beadsman, wan and pale,
Masked in frozen hood and mail,
Turns aloft his sunken eye
As he tells his rosary;
Thus they sought and found their home
Underneath some leafy dome,
Where many an ancient altar stood
Steaming with its recent blood.

Nor deemed they that each fawn and fay,
Like ghosts alarmed, would flit away
When the sun rose at dawn of day.
But within each grove and dell
A light upon their darkness fell;
Glancing through each giant tree
Silently and suddenly.
Then these vagrants trembling fled,
Filled with more than mortal dread;
Or, dissolved in mist and air,
Muttering words of deep despair,
On they went to regions dire,
As wolves retreating from the fire
When every herb and bush and spire
Leaves the blasted prairie bare.

Old Thor knit his angry brow,
Made in haste a desperate vow,
That, with hammer in his hand,
Over the sea and over the land,
He would send one spark,—a scathing brand,

The last of all his missiles spent;
And where it fell, or whither it went,
He little cared, if he might know
It dealt a deep and deadly blow;
For well he knew his power would end
With the last bolt his arm would send.

Here Odin, with his giant seers,
And his shivering ice-bound peers,
With eyes afrozen, dull, and dim,
Which could not in their sockets swim,
Now wept a few big drops, that fell
Within the ocean's angry swell,
And, ever since, each icy spur
That northward checks the mariner—
Those mountain masses that float along
In fathomless fiords, heavy and strong—
Remind him of those days of yore
When he the frozen sceptre bore
Along old Norway's horrid shore.

The God-wish Aiger, in despair,
Aloud exclaimed, "Now have a care!"
And in a sullen storm, that woke
His slumbers by a sudden stroke,
Cried, "Save the ship! cut every spar!
There's neither light of sun or star;
We are floating to a world afar!"
And, seizing on the helm, which broke
With too heavy a hand and stroke,
He perished in the stormy wave,
And found a deep and darksome grave,
And none to pity, none to save!

Thus, the whole fabled race,
In confusion and fear,
Will abashed hide their face,
And at length disappear,
At the sound of that word
By the nations once heard.
And now, shunning the light,
To the regions of night

As outcasts they fly
To seek shelter and die;
Or, with demons of old,
Scorched with fires, or left shivering with
snow drifts acold.

II.

At the birth of old Time,
When fresh in her prime,
Like the heavens sublime,
The earth was all beauty, without sin or pain,
And the slime of the serpent had left not one
stain;
It is said that the angels held converse with those
Who sought their repose
'Neath the shade of that tree;—
The new Igdrasil, which forever shall be,
To hear the sweet notes of their rich melody.

Softly they breathed to the listening ear
Strains which 'twere madness now to hear.

Such notes should their lips to our senses give
birth,
The heavens would descend to the dwellers on
earth,
And the soul would be drowned by their awful
mirth!
In pity to mortals, their voices are mute,
And silent each harp-string and heavenly lute.
The chorals that break from a thousand spheres
Die ere they reach our leaden ears,
Or seem like the bells of the flowers that chime
To the monads that nestle in beds of thyme!

But how blest was that pair,
Such communion to share!
How honored their lot
And sacred each spot!
How hallowed each visit, and tender their love,
When the bright shining ones from the regions
above
Partook of their pleasure,
Unalloyed, without measure.

With no thought of to-morrow,
No care, and no sorrow!
More bright than a dream
In life's freshest stream,
When the soul with the richest of fancies may
teem.
'Twas a birth
On the earth
Such as angels might covet, but never could feel,
Which the bowers of Eden to them did reveal.

Not a thing to bewail
As a love-lorn tale,—
The hero a knave, or a worthless snail,
Whom the world would not miss, if he had died,
More than a leaf on the swollen tide,—
A phosphor light,
Born of putrescence,—a thing to affright;
But a love that came
Like a vestal flame,
Rosy and warm
And without alarm;

More subtle and bright than our goldenest dreams,
And purer than all the fabled streams
That run through Elysian fields on high,
To bathe in which it were heaven to die!
But a love to us poor mortals given
        From the innermost heaven;
        Pure as the ray
          Which from yonder sun
        On the waters play
          Or the mountains dun.
Warm as the heat of a summer's noon,
Chaste as the light of a full-orbed moon;
        'Twas a word of bliss
Of more than mortal blessedness.
        All that was bright
        In heaven's own light;—
        All that is fair
        With it we compare,
And we call it a thing more rich and rare.
        All that is sweet,
        And all that is meet
To measure our heart's wish and make it complete.

But how changed was the scene, when, with guilt
and with shame,
To the tree of existence, surrounded with flame,
Forbidden to come or to taste of its fruit,
While the angels, astonished, stood silent and
mute!

All the air was then burdened with sobs and
with sighs,
And tears fell as rain from those pitying
eyes,
Unused until then to that amber-rich dew
Which the heart crushed with sorrow now
brings into view.

Sudden wails swept the branches, as winds sweep
the sail
Borne along by the might of a desperate gale;
And, as far as the ear could detect, now there
grew
Distant sounds faint, yet fainter, and whispering,
"Adieu."

Through the ocean in which our lone earth moves
along,
Myriad voices aloft bore this word, loud and
strong;
And, till reaching the portals of sunshine and
day,
The sound still was heard on their sad lips to
stay.

To the listening vaults and the sky-arching
dome,
Where the bright-wingéd beings were hastening
home,
Their answering echoes were sent fresh as dew
To that burdened refrain, murmuring only,
"Adieu."

And the word floats aloft, as if wingéd with fire,
To the innermost Temple, the altar and choir;
And the sound shapes the voices, now faintly
and dim,
Of the bright-vested cherubs, the rapt seraphim.

Ever since, mid the tree of existence, is heard
Through its sunlight and shadows, this sorrowful
word;
And when nipt by the frost, red and sallow and
sear,
Its leaves fall to dust, 'tis the last sound they
hear.

III.

O man, pause and pray!
Be admonished to-day,
When pleasure is nigh,
When the earth is all freshness,—all splendor
the sky.
Now a smile, then a tear,
A foe may appear,
Which may turn all thy joyance to anguish and
fear.
Then the rain-drops are shed
O'er the path that you tread,
And nothing to shelter the pitiless head.

Darkness and doubt
Within and without;
Anguish and sorrow,
To-day and to-morrow;
Guilt for the past
Which forever may last.
This is death, worse than death, to the sin-stricken soul;
It has driven ten thousand unwashed to their goal.
But hope sheds its fragrance upon the crushed heart,
And the joy of the Lord bids each sorrow depart.
Then, one smile from his face, howe'er dark be the night,
Will dispel all its shadows and turn them to light.

IV.

Is it the breath of a human sigh,
A floating leaf as it passeth by?

A tear that is falling upon a stone
From a heart that is breaking all alone?

Is it a pang that none may share?
The wail of a spirit in deep despair,
Seeking relief, and it knows not where?
    Look upwards and see,
    Ere the visions flee.
O'er the dull beaten path in which we now tread,
Where the fruits that we gather with ashes are
    spread,
Hope wings her bright pinions and bends her
    meek head.

V.

Toil we here, both night and day,
    To win a name
    That will not stay,
In chase of that phantom that men call fame.
    Hungry as night,
    Watchful as light;

Through marsh and through glen,
We eager pursue
What, in gaining, we rue.
Though the soul be lost,
Or by passion tost;
And we barter all
At its clarion call;
Still onward we move,
As if madly to prove
That life is the gleam of the meteor's light,
And fame, but the sound as it fades from the sight.
The hopes of our youth,
What are they, in truth,
But memories now?
The flowers are all faded,
The garlands are braided,
And withered they lie,
Pale as ashes, and dry.
The future, which sheds such a light on our path,
Is the mirage that mocks us in anger and wrath.

VI.

Pleasure and mirth
Have an unquiet birth;
And frail
Is their life as a passing gale.
They come to us here
From a higher sphere.
They come, like birds from a sunny clime,
Where their voices blend as the bells in a chime
At a marriage feast,
Where the waiting priest
Is ready to make two hearts sublime.
But they will not stay:
In a moment away,
Chilled by the blasts of a wintry day.
Let us suffer and do,
As we onward pursue
What is best for us here.

'Tis my faith and trust,
That, whatever befall,
It were better that dust
On our bright hopes might fall,
Than fail to be ready at duty's stern call.

VII.

Through the shadows and gloom which enshroud
us above,
One eye still looks on us, of pity and love;
And I know that, whatever disturbs now my
breast,
There's a home for the weary,—a haven of rest.

With a conscience unstained, and a heart firm
and pure,
We may laugh at our ills, and all trials endure,
Borne above all the changes of birth and of
blood,
The waves and the surges of passion's dark
flood.

To existence—the future, the present, the past—
I am bound by a chain that forever will last,
That no power can destroy, no rust can consume:
'Tis the gift which survives all the wrecks of the tomb.

Its links are all golden, and forged by a hand,
Which in nicest adjustment and beauty are planned;
And though melted, and beaten, and welded in fire,
'Tis to bring out their brightness and raise it still higher.

Life is greater than food: he who gave us this boon
Will not leave us to perish before it is noon;
The greater includes all the lesser:—then know
He who gave us this pearl, smaller gems will bestow.

The past we have conquered, and we smile at
its toils,
Reassured by its conflicts, enriched by its spoils;
The future though darkly its shadows display,
Yet "sufficient the evil" that comes with each
day.

VIII.

It is our life that changes; sense
Deceives not: still we draw from thence
Our wayward fancies and our fond conceits,
And hide us in their intricate retreats.
Blindly we look, or shut the opened ear,
And yield our hearts to folly and to fear.

The world surrounds us like a wall of fire,
Or fetters with its chains ice-cold and dire:
Through its wide ramparts none of us can
pierce,
Though with fixed eyes we gaze, like eagles
fierce.

Beyond, our senses never caught a ray
Save that which mingles with the common day.
Yet is it real; and no power can bind
Its influence o'er the ever restless mind.

The seasons come and go; the sun shines on:
Whether we smile or weep, his race is won.
The grass still springs, the freshened turf still
blows
With wakened flowers; earth has its many
throes.
The oak still lifts its ancient form on high,
And stars display their glorious heraldry.

Here stands our home, within the forest dell,
In shade and sunshine;—there the plashing well.
Crimson and clear, the beams upon it rest,
Or clouds and tempests shake its quiet breast;
And tinkling streams keep music to the hour,
When evening comes, to show its gentle power.
Or when the wintry sky, in shroud or snow;
Or on the purple peaks the sunsets glow;

Or battling tempests swell the turbid floods,
Or the rough north winds shake its naked woods,
Nature, unchanging, mocks our idle moods.

Familiar scenes,—these change not, but abide;
Our bark but varies with the onward tide.
The very tombs, where dust and ashes lie,
Seem like the fixtures of eternity.
Here in the rocks the hordes of Egypt sleep,
And, like the mountains hoar, their relics keep;
As if a part of those eternal walls,
And built to keep them ever in their halls.

Where shall we anchor hopes that will not fail,
Or whither hasten with our storm-rent sail?
Is there no life beyond, no future rest,
No peace for weary feet or throbbing breast?
Imprisoned here, we sigh to wing our way
To realms beyond the light of common day.

With joys above the shadows of a dream,
The wildering senses with fond fancies teem.

And earthly loves have power the soul to shake
With tones of ravishment, that make
Us feel how feeble and how vain
Are earth's endeavors to allay our pain,
To help our discontent, to chain our grief,
To send the burdened spirit sweet relief.

Oh, there are moments when with guilt and
wrong,
Dark dreams and passions dire, our spirits
throng;
When, sad and weary, the o'erburdened breast
Bows like the willow when by floods oppressed;
Haunted by memories, whence unbidden start
Thoughts, elf-like, from the chambers of the
heart:
No magic power their presence can surprise,
No spells can charm, nor words can exorcise.

PART THIRD.

I.

Not all of truth do we yet believe,
Nor all that is final the wisest receive;
Its massive shadows now hide from our sight
Much that is found in the realms of light.

Glints of sunshine fall on our way;
Wandering beams on our footsteps play,
Like those which fall on an April day;
But the summer will come, and a brighter sky
Will dawn on our pathway and shine on high.

O heart by the tempests strangely driven,
On the headlands of doubt so rudely riven;
Yet know that the treasures, in depths that lie
In the caverns below, will be swept on high
And soon will appear to thy anxious eye.

No types, howe'er perfect, have ever expressed
All the light and resplendence which gleam
from the breast
Of the vestment which Truth in her jewelled
shrine
Has placed on the heart by a hand divine.

No dogmas of prelates or priests can bind
The thoughts which leap forth from the un-
fettered mind;
For the truth will be seen, as a beacon on
high,
Through the rack of the storm-cloud which
darkens the sky.

Steady shining, though hidden at times by the
shade,
It seems like an angel our fancy has made;
Rounding out in its beauty, at length 'twill
appear,
When from mists and from tempests the sky
shall be clear,

And in brightness shall walk o'er the pavement
of blue,
To shed on our pathway its radiant hue.

II.

Brave hearts, true as brave,
Battling hard for the right,
Have gone down to the grave
In the noblest of fight;
And their blood has been shed,
Like the water as free
From the clouds overhead,
Which now fall in the sea.
But the bravest in woman at duty's stern call;
For the fight of her faith is the noblest of
all.

In the darkest of days,
In proud temples she stood,
And no offerings of praise,
And no victims of blood,

No vows and no gifts, at even or morn,
To the shrine of an idol by her hands would
be borne.

Not one grain would she bring
As a false offering;
Not one rite would perform
Though the gathering storm,
Red and lowering with blood,
Might be calmed and subdued.

Her faith rose sublime
Over passion and crime,
Giving courage to weakness
And manhood to meekness;
And an arm, though unseen,
On which fainting to lean;
And a power ever nigh,
On which to rely,
Upholding, sustaining the earth and the sky.
No favor she sought,
No worship she brought,

Save to Him who had loved her and taught her
to know
How rich is that peace which his blood can
bestow;
Who is worthy alone to receive from the
heart
All the homage and love which the soul can
impart;
Who had taught her to die, than to fail to
express
The truth which his followers are called to
confess.

Yes, 'tis better to die
Than to strangle in birth
The free thoughts which cry
For deliverance on earth.

Far better the prison, the iron, the sword,
Than to quench but one spark of the God-given
word:

The seed-thoughts once uttered a harvest may
win
Of souls now polluted, from folly and sin.

Our great Leader confessed, and o'er truth's
sacred shrine
He poured out his blood as an offering divine;
And he taught us this lesson:—ye craven hearts,
hear!
"He who fears the One Father, no one else need
he fear."

SONG.

ANCIENT GREEK MARTYRS.

Lord of the worlds above,
To thee we humbly bow;
The martyr's crown we seek;
Place it upon our brow!

No "Io Pæan!" rings
Upon the burdened air

From us, who once could shout
  Songs to Aurora fair.

Apollo hears not now
  The joyful maidens' chaunt,
In cypress grove or glen,
  Where wood-nymphs used to haunt.

No music from our lips,
  At shadowy eve along,
Fills Daphne's bowers dim
  With wild voluptuous song.

Phœbus, at early dawn,
  Looks not for us to bring
The dewy freshened flowers,
  Or costly offering.

Not to an idol's shrine
  We lowly bend the knee;
But to thine altars, Lord,
  We come; we come to thee!

Lamb that was slain for us;
  Son, that to us was given,
Earth is all stained with sin:—
  Our home is heaven.

Earth groans with many a pang;
  Signs fill the darkened air;
Come, with thy festal robes
  Thy waiting bride prepare.

The thousand ages bring
  The expectant jubilee!
The scattered tribes still wait:
  They wait for thee!

III.

"How long?" was the wild, the piercing cry
Which swept the earth and cleaved the sky,
When blood like water was freely poured
At the feet of thine altars, mighty Lord!

In the depths of their sorrow and heavy
woe,
The "first-born" then felt its terrible throe;
And the "just made perfect" were summoned
to share
The conflict their brethren were doomed to
bear.

Like the kingdoms of earth,
When a star of their own
Is strangled at birth,—
Into darkness thrown.
At the trumpet's clang,
Every warrior bold,
As its echoes rang
Through his mountain-hold,
Will leap to his steed,
And, with eager speed,
The feeblest, the meekest,
The mightiest, the weakest,
Will rush to the fight
To defend the right;

And the pride of their forces, the young and
the fair,
To the conflict now summoned, in haste will
prepare,
And hurl their dread missiles of wrath and of
woe
'Gainst the haughty invader, the insolent foe.

IV.

In the struggle and strife
Through the ages now fled,
Soaked and crimsoned with life,
Lie the fields of the dead.
The grass and the turf
Have been swept by the surf
Of the Red Sea of battle, that breaks on the
land,
Leaving its stains on the white drifted sand.

By infection and death,
And murder's foul breath,

The air is defiled
With "the heaps upon heaps" packed, and
pressed down, and piled;
Choking rivers and streams,
Till the rotten mass steams
Hot with fervors which blight
All that is touched by the horrible sight.

In the rivers that glide
In their beauty and pride;
In the ocean's wave,
They have found a grave,
With their martial cloaks so grand,
Filled and ballasted with sand;
Wrecked and ruined now they lie
'Neath the calm and quiet sky!

V.

Like a ship's crew, safe and warm,
Fearing neither wind nor storm;

Dreaming long and sweet of home,
As o'er oceans wide they roam,
Till a treacherous sea ahead
Sends them all within a bed
Where the furies feed and gloat
On the carcasses that float.
And the sea-swell's angry breast,
With its furious, foaming crest,
Bears them like a worthless weed,
Or a frail and shattered reed,
Far upon the beetling shore,
Stunned by its everlasting roar.

Dark the night, and ill the guide,
When the vessel in its pride
Struck the breakers; and how soon
All went down, as in a swoon,
'Neath the watery, waning moon!

See! the captain helpless yields,
Who had won a hundred fields,

To the ceaseless waves, that leave
Lance and bearer at each heave:
'Tis enough to make one grieve!

In his wildly-floating hair,
In his eyes, which blindly stare,
The brine has left its deadly stain,
Which all the floods cannot wash again.

VI.

Oft have I seen the purple even
Burdened with the quickening levin;
Far away in the western heaven.
I have watched the sun go down
Over the fields and over the town;
And the one bright star, with many stars
Were sailing aloft, like silver cars;
Shining like molten furnaces,
Or jewels upon a bridal dress.

Their liquid light
Was like phosphor bright,
Or the eye of an iron steed, at night.
All in a glow,
Like the flowers that blow
In the breath of June,
Were the stars overhead, and the full-orbed moon.

VII.

The wind crept up the secret glen,
Along the streams and the sedgy fen.
The rippling waves ran down the brook,
And the coarse grass curved, and the marsh-moor shook;
And the tall trees lifted their branches high,
Bathed in the light of a summer sky.
The owlet hid from the moon's pale beams,
And the whip-poor-will glided along the streams.
The silent bat clove the yielding air,
And the sky and the earth seemed wondrous fair.

Then I asked the winds, "Say, whence have ye
come?
And whither ye seek your chosen home?"
"We come from the line of the Southern
Cross,
Where the foaming waves still tumble and
toss;
And we found a ship, as still as death;
Not a wave was stirred by a passing breath.
Her sails were hanging loose and lank,
And the juice was oozing from every plank;
And the lazy crew were asleep in the hold,
Like sheep now gathered within the fold.
All were silent as silence could be,—
The ship, and the crew, and the glassy sea.
And I hid myself in a cloud at hand,
That Hesper had borne from a distant land.
Then I struck the sea into phosphor flame,
And the quivering bark, that bore the name
Of the 'Ocean Wave,' fifty fathoms deep
Went down to the weeds, where the zoophytes
sleep.

Oh, 'twas a sight so grand, to see
That ship, with its doomèd company,
Sink, and no threatening reef nigh or lea!
The helmsman awoke and clung to a spar,
And was driven a hundred knots afar,
No sun by day, and by night no star.

"Seven days' famine and thirst and fright,
I beheld him there, in his wretched plight.
In pity I sent a thundering hail,
And I beat him down with my icy flail;
And along my track I have left the wreck
Of many a broken, floundering deck.
And now I am weary, and slowly creep
Up the reedy marshes, to take my sleep
Far away from the stormy deep."

VIII.

By falsehood's foul breath,
Scattering arrows and death,
The air is polluted and vile.

It were well if the torch
Were applied to the porch
To consume, with a touch, the huge pile;
That the chambers which hide,
In their glitter and pride,
All deception, and error, and cant,
Might be routed and cleared,
And the walls scorched and seared,
Without notice of *courier avant.*

For ages the temple in mockery has stood,
Defiled by the lust of its votaries, and blood;
And, though covered with tinsel, and gleaming
with light,
Within, all is ghastly and gloomy as night.
And as truth has its temple, its altar, its priests,
Its gifts and its worship, its fasts and its feasts,
Its father, its children, its honors, its gains,
So falsehood its orgies, its patrons, its fanes.
Both the sweet and the bitter we press to our
lips;
Every form has its shadow,—the sun its eclipse.

And if Christ has an empire he claims as his own,
So Satan his kingdom, his sceptre, his throne.
Each his army, in numbers as leaves in the air
When the eddying winds lay the forest all bare.

IX.

Fear not, though the scowl
Of defiance and scorn
On his brow fierce and foul
By the base fiend is borne.
Mighty powers are nigh
To aid thee to win
Rich spoils for the sky
Over death, hell, and sin;
And the smile of thy foe,
Like the meteor's light,
But a moment will glow,
Then dissolve into night.

Now, clad in their armor of glory and pride,
From their coverts they rush, like a dark swollen tide;
Defiant and bold, richly covered with mail,
And armed with keen arrows and furious as hail.
Their hosts fill the air and darken the sky,
With wings tipped with lightning so swiftly they fly;
And, the air filled with portents, they eagerly scour
Every nook, every quarter, their foes to devour.

Though mid leaves of the Igdrasil now they retire,
And send forth their arrows all gleaming with fire,
To corrupt every passion, inflame every lust,
And to lay all that's beautiful low in the dust,
Yet in God will we conquer: his shield is our trust.

Though their breath stirs the tempests that howl
round the tree,
As erewhile on the waves of the dark Gal-
lilee;
And its branches are severed and tossed in the
air,
'Tis but wrath roused by weakness, the might
of despair.

And though famine, with eyes sunken deeply
and dim,
And death, its dark shadow, follows silent and
grim,
And lust, with its eyes as the basilisk bright,
Stalks abroad as at midnight, and hating the
light,
Our Leader will put them to shame and affright.

And though feuds they engender, and war to
the knife,
In the church, in the state, stirring hatred and
strife,

And hand joined in hand for the conflict prepare,
Madly bent on the spoils of the fallen to share;
And passion and hatred they scatter as seed,
A harvest of incest and murder to breed,
An arm still is ready in seasons of need.

X.

The bright shining ones, in their vestments so
fair,
Still encircle this tree as it waves through the air;
And their wings scatter odors and blossoms
around,
Enriching the air and o'erspreading the ground.

Since creation's first dawn have they watched
o'er the earth,
As they sang the first song on the morn of its
birth;
And as swift and as silent as arrows of light,
They glance through the air in their rapturous
flight.

Shapes of brightness and beauty, they watch o'er
the pure,
And endow them with courage and strength to
endure
All the malice and hatred, all the pain and the
woe,
Devised by their recreant, desperate foe.

What sounds of rich melody fall on the ear,
In the soul's inward senses, mellifluous and
clear,
As the conflict grows sterner, with hearts firm
and true,
They resolve still to battle, to suffer and do!

XI.

Founts of hidden pleasure,
Without stint or measure,
Are to them unsealed,
And shapes of wondrous beauty to the eye
revealed!

Words of love
From above,
Voices soundless,
Joyous, boundless;
Hosts in armor bright
Stretching onward, from the earth, to the gates
of light!

Visions brighter than a dream
Now before their senses gleam;
Brighter than that weary one
Had when, at the setting sun,
On the ground he made his bed,
Pillowing with a stone his head.
Mantled in his cloak, he lay
Till the dawning of the day:
While he dreamed, a ladder swung
Pendant, from the stars among,
Farther than the eye could see
In the realms of purity.
Thence, descending
And ascending,

Watchers passed the star-paved night
Till the dawning of the light.

Oh, these dwellers old!
Through the night drear and cold,
Mid the darkness and the shame,
Mid the torturing rack and flame,
Still they come, as once they came,
Walking to and fro the earth,
Since creation's glorious birth;
Noiselessly they hither trip,
Fondly seeking fellowship,
In our lone and circling sphere,
With the race of dwellers here;
And, with many a rapturous song,
Bear the joyful news along
Of the tears which drown the sense
In the seas of penitence.

Where the fatted kid is slain
For the dead, alive again,

And the seething embers burn
At the prodigal's return,
Joining in the song and glee
Of the great festivity;

Or amid the choice retreat
Where the pure and faithful meet,
Joying to behold them raise
Prayer for help, or songs of praise;
Or, offended, turn away,
And to brighter regions stray,
When unseemly rites and vile
Taint the burdened air the while.

XII.

Where the verdure and the bloom,
Fresh upon the recent tomb
Of the dædal earth was seen,
Washed by the flood of waters clean,
Oft they came, and sought their way
Where the feet of pilgrims stray;

And in human form and face,
Humble garb, and saintly grace,
They would seek refreshment, ease
In the tent, beneath the trees;
And receive both rest and fare,
Princely feasts, and grateful care.

Or where bold impiety
Armed the thunderbolts on high,
And the gathering, angry levin
Muttered words of wrath in heaven,
Sped they quick to guard and warn,
Weak and helpless and forlorn,
Those who suffered, wept, and prayed,
And on God for mercy staid.

XIII.

Ere the fiery tempest lowers
On the doomèd city's towers;
On its walls and gates of brass,
Its crowded streets, through which now pass

Those who buy and those who sell,
Those who in proud mansions dwell,
And the poor, the base, the mean,
In the busy marts were seen.
Vassals, with their haughty lords,
Despots, with their hungry hordes.
The rich, who proudly, stately tread,
And the poor, who beg for bread;
Men, who seek themselves to please,
Women, careless and at ease;
On they move, nor dream the day
Which arose so bright and gay
Such a tempest could display.

Not a cloud to dim its light,
Not a portent to affright,
Not a distant gleam of ire,
Not a bolt of hidden fire,
Not a murmur to inspire
Thought of danger or alarm,
Death, or fear of any harm.

None, in fancy's seer-like gleams,
None, in faint prophetic dreams,
Could anticipate the doom
Which should wrap their homes in gloom
In a fiery, smouldering tomb.

XIV.

In the sultry noon of day,
Where the tents of Abram lay,
On the plains of Mamre seen,
Travel-worn, in humble mien,
Came now three, and by him stood,
Wanderers over field and flood.

Rising from his chosen seat,
Low he bows him at their feet.
"Let thy servant now, I pray,
Beg you will not hence away
Till a basin I shall bring
Dripping from the gushing spring;

And aweary, as 'tis meet,
I shall wash your dusty feet.
Rest you here beneath this tree
Till refreshed by mine and me;
Comfort here your hearts with bread,
Ere from hence your way is sped:"
They replied, "Do as thou'st said."

XV.

"Quickly bake three measures fine
Of the meal, whilst from the kine
I select the choicest, best,
And with milk and curdles dressed,
We prepare a fit repast,
Ere the sun its shadows cast:"
Then beneath the sheltering tree
Here they sat,—the strangers three.

XVI.

"Where is Sarah now, thy wife,
She, the partner of thy life?"

In the tent, behold, she stands,
Busy with her thrifty hands.
Then One said,—divine his air,
Face, and form, beyond compare,—
"I will certainly return
Unto thee, what time shall burn
In the socket, pale and dim,
Life in quivering heart and limb;
And, ere your work on earth is done,
Sarah shall bear to you a son."
Within she heard, nor could express
Half that she felt, but would suppress;
She laughed, not loud, in spirit low,—
Laughed but to think it should be so!
"Now, wherefore did she laugh?" said he;
"Is any thing too hard for ME?
Yet, at the time appointed, know
The promised boon I will bestow."
"I laughed not," Sarah, trembling, said:
Weak was her faith, and sore afraid.
"Nay, thou didst laugh," he quick replied,—
And with this word, they onward hied.

XVII.

In the rich fields where Sodom lay
The herdsman Lot had found his way:
Selfish and weak, he eager went
To pitch in Siddim's vale his tent.

To him well known on every hand
The wicked dwellers in the land;
Cautious at first to mix with those,
Known to be his and Abram's foes.

Too near to escape the tempter's wiles,
His fascination and his smiles;
And soon he seeks the city's walls,
Leaving his tent for princely halls.

Entangled by his social ties
And many a bait of sweet surprise,
Familiar with the scenes around,
By chains of custom Lot is bound.

Though vexed his righteous soul each day,
Too faint to leave, afraid to stay,
Too just to approve, to weak to run,
He mourned the sin he dared not shun;

Nor courage had, nor any grace,
To free him from the tainted place,
But found companionship and shame
With those who scorned Jehovah's name!

Peril and trial none can fly;
Sin and its brood are ever nigh:
Yet rather fly to deserts waste
Than seek its poisonous fruits to taste.

XVIII.

At eventide the herdsman sate
Near to the city's open gate;
When, lo! two stately forms appear,
To whom, with reverence, Lot drew near.

"My lords, I pray you, stay this night
Within my house, till morning light,
And, ere the sun has blessed the day,
Rise and pursue your onward way."
"Nay, in the street will we abide:
No evils will to us betide."
Lot pressed them hard. Within the door
Shelter they found, and ample store.

XIX.

The horrors of that night, for shame,
We dare not speak, we will not name:
Let it suffice that wrath apace
Was threatened 'gainst the dooméd place.
"Up! fly thee from these hated walls;
Thou and thy sons, forsake its halls."
And while they lingered, hand to hand,
They force them from the sin-cursed land.
"Haste, for thy life; look not behind;
Dead be to all you leave, and blind!

Fly to the mountains whence you came,
Or perish in the wrathful flame!"

XX.

The sun rose clear that day on high,
And not a cloud bedimmed the sky,
And, bathed within its yellow light,
Cities and plains shone wondrous bright;
When God rained fire from heaven, to brand
All that was seen upon the land.
Cities and plains, and flocks and men,
Doomed ne'er to rise on earth again.

Thus ever round our path they stray,
To guide and guard us in our way;
Though now unseen, a watchful eye
Still sends these warders from the sky.
In sickness, sorrow, guilt, and shame,
They gird us by a wall of flame;
In pain and anguish of the mind,
They guard us, viewless as the wind.

Darkness and doubt before them flee,
On the verge of life's deep mystery;
And outward sorrow or despair
Flee by their presence into air.
In prisons, tortures, rack, and flame,
In sorrow, suffering, and in shame,
In deserts wild or mountains drear,
In doubt and darkness, hope and fear,
Or on the earth or on the sea,
They come in our extremity;
And, by some wakened thought or word,
Or inward feeling strongly stirred,
They move, admonish, cherish, fill,
Our plastic spirits at their will.

PART FOURTH.

I.

LIKE Egypt, dark uprose a spell
From the murky depths of hell;
The smoke-smothered air was thick and dun
Up to the central sun.

Chaos again, and ancient night,
Drunk every shimmering ray of light;
And dim-eyed workers, gaunt and pale,
Moved like the oozy snail.

Like the salt that licks the shore,
Leaving it baser than before;
So the sea of darkness rose and fell
With a mighty swell.

Men were affrighted, in terror fled,
Weary with life, and sought the dead;
Drenched with the rain and heartless sea,
Mad with their misery!

Its waves were breaking upon the strand,
Over the ramparts, over the land,
Over the hamlets, the hill-clad vines,
Over the storm-tost pines;

The hoary woods, and the waving grain,
And cities that smoked along the plain,
And the gem-like cots that slumbering lie
Neath the quiet sky

Where the children played at dusky eve,
And the homeward flocks a pathway weave;
And the social swallow skimmed the air,
When the night was fair.

II.

Oh, it was cold as cold could be,
And dark as cold, on that swollen sea;
The sun seemed dying in his own blood,
And in terror stood.

And the stars grew pale, and the watery moon
Reeled and faded, as in a swoon;
And the thunder-split hills, by earthquakes riven,
Into the floods were driven.

And the earth grew faint for the wretched sight,
And sighed for one ray of the morning light;
And the dial receded full fifty degrees
And left her to freeze.

III.

Then, as wild beasts come forth from their coverts
to roam,
With eyes flashing fire, and teeth white with foam,

When the mantle of night o'er the forest is
spread,—
So the lawless by passion and instinct were led.

In its deepening shade they hunted their spoil,
And the dead and the living polluted the soil;
And the blood of their victims, like rain, soaked
the earth,
And the air was oppressed with their maniac-
mirth.

Horrid forms of humanity dwelt in the shade,
And gods, fierce and cruel, their own hands had
made;
And the bones of old heroes and saints long
entombed,
In their mad superstition, they eager exhumed.

Wooden crosses they wore on their necks and
their hands,
Which, alas! were soon changed into batons and
brands;

And with these they beat down and consumed every foe,
Till the earth groaned and maddened in anguish and woe.

Wearied out with their sorrows, borne down by their waves,
Men fled to the deserts and hid in their caves,
And sought in their solitudes respite from fear,
Mid the crags and the Alpine cliffs horrid and drear.

But they bore with them safely the leaves of that tree
Which from sickness and sorrow would set them all free;
And the lamp that was lit at the altars of love,
Burning brightly they kept, fed with oil from above.

And while darkness still brooded upon the vile
race
Who the pure faith in Christ from the world
would efface,
In the rude Alpine hills, like the light of a star,
Was a Pharos, which shone through the ages afar.

IV.

Ten centuries—a decade most direful and drear,
Full of carnage and guilt, brooding terror and
fear—
Moved on like the tramp of a conquering foe,
Leaving nothing behind them but ruin and woe.

The earth groaned beneath them, the skies
darkly lowered,
Ere the gathering tempests upon them were
poured,
When the Saracen forces, with rapine and pride,
Swept the land with the might of their deep
crimson tide.

With the fierceness of lions, the fleetness of fire,
With the stings of the scorpion all burning with
ire,
Both by fraud and by force, with the rack and
the sword,
They devoured the apostates, by Heaven ab-
horred.

Ever thus has it been when the truth has been
slain,
And no power save the sword may revive it
again;
Then "to arms" is the cry, when from earth
peace has fled,
And pity her last tear of sorrow has shed.

Now a nation as vile as the one it invades
Will be mustered to battle and draw its bright
blades,
And the "potsherds of earth" with their equals
contend,
And the powers above all their influence lend.

V.

As the light shines more brightly, more perfect
the day,
So the shadows more deeply their gloom will
display;
And as mercy its fulness of blessing reveals,
Behind her injustice more covertly steals;

Thus the power of evil we never can know
Till good all its riches of kindness shall
show;
As the spectres of darkness our spirits affright
When the gleam of the sunshine our prisons
may light.

When the true prophets came, then the false
ones were near,
When the Christ, then the anti-Christ soon will
appear;

So the base coin is seen without measure or stint
When the good in abundance shall pour from
the mint.

VI.

As the child in its helplessness needs every stay
To guard and defend it along its new way,
So, when weak in its infancy, God wisely gave
Signs and wonders, the church from all error to
save.

But when instinct gives place to a far nobler
guide,
And reason stands by us, and clings to our side,
Then the age filled with portents shall hence
pass away,
For the mind needs but truth for its prop and
its stay.

But, as man is both foolish and false to his race,
Idle tales, endless fables, his records disgrace;

And the pure light of heaven by them soon will
pale,
And darkness and error instead will prevail.

"Lying wonders and signs" fill the earth and
the sky,
And Madonnas a-weeping pump up tears to each
eye;
Januarius at Naples, as old as the Flood
And as dry as a mummy, still shows running
blood.

Saintly bones and old cloaks, ragged shirts and
old shoes,
Holy relics and medals, will not even refuse
To perform wondrous cures, and to raise e'en
the dead;
So the church of the priesthood has piously said.

And to rescue the sepulchre out of the hand
Of the Moslem, who claims still his share in the
land

Which the prophets and martyrs received as
their own,
And which Israel in fee holds the title alone

All Europe was summoned, the young and the old,
The weak and the mighty, the timid and bold;
To unite all their forces in one mighty stream,
Of merit sufficient, their souls to redeem!

Moved by heaven, it was said, boys and girls
stole away;
In battalions they hastened as suppliants to pray
That the "Virgin Immaculate" now would
restore
The only sure way to the kingdom,—this door!

On the Alps, amid famine and ice-cliffs and sleet,
Thirty thousand were seen without shoes on
their feet,
And were dragged or were driven, like sheep, to
be slain,
The rock-girded sepulchre thus to obtain.

Even now, in our own chosen home in the West,
Mother-church deems herself highly honored
and blest
To invite all her children without fail to come
And hold in Saint Xavier a grand *Triduum.*

PETER CLAVER.

Due honors now by saintly Xavier
Are given to ancient Peter Claver,
A canonized saint of Nono Pio,
And henceforth known within Ohio
As one who centuries past had died,
But only now beatified!

O pious Claver! what a story
Could you relate of Purgatory,
Since the fell day that you were tired
Of this vain world, and then expired!
It was too bad that you should wait
So long a time at Peter's gate,

Ere in his realms to slip or slide,
And join the saints, beatified!

You doubtless thought it very long
Ere you had joined the happy throng,
When others guiltier far, and meaner,
Had gone, than Peter of Cargena;
In truth, I guess they were disguised,
And stole among the canonized.

But merit, soon or late, is sure
To be requited to the pure;
And though forgotten and neglected,
Perchance proscribed, or else suspected,
At length has come the unlooked-for favor
To poor, desponding Peter Claver.
A *Triduum* is here begun
In honor of the fame you won;
In which your deeds of great renown
Are heralded through all the town:
How that, with many other things
As mother-church his praises sings,

Diseases of the sick he bore;
The blind to sight he did restore;
And even to life he raised the dead,
As fame, with doubtful tongue, has said.

His cloak—though worn and very old,
Used to defend him from the cold—
He oft was known to kindly spread
Beneath the dying and the dead;
Though not so full of virtue then,
As when on earth a denizen
Old Clavier lived; but, from the hour
He died, with some strange power
The sick by contact it will save,
And snatch even victory from the grave.
And now it is by Rome decreed,
The faithful shall from sin be freed,
And full indulgence shall be given
To trample on the laws of heaven,
If this *Triduum*, without waver,
Shall now be kept for Peter Claver.

And prayer for Christian kings be given,
To Him that rules o'er earth and heaven,
That concord shall with them be found
To crush each free thought to the ground;
To quench each spark of generous fire
The breath of freedom may inspire,
And thus to exorcise and free
The world from hateful heresy,
And so exalt the church on high
Above the earth, above the sky,
That all the poor, the rich, the great,
Of every kingdom, realm, and state,
Shall learn submissively to bow
To him upon whose awful brow
Was placed long since the triple crown,
To crush the truth and keep it down
Beneath his fierce and withering frown.
And thus is heard this strange palaver,
Within the halls of sainted Xavier,
About this priest, old Peter Claver.

PART FIFTH.

I.

SEE now what stately temples stand,
With jewels brought from every land;
And chief are those to Mammon raised,
Whose altars every age have praised
'Neath the Igdrasil.
Under this tree, within the mould,
In search of that bauble that men call gold,
They are digging still,—
Digging and delving, day and night,
To bring the yellow dust to light;
The feet of the beautiful, hands of the brave,
Forsaking all, its treasures to crave.

Dig! dig! dig!
Churchman, Tory, and Whig,
Old and young, the little and big;

With mattock and spade and hoe,
With hoe and mattock and spade!
The rich and the poor of every grade,
    Are bending low
    To delve, delve, delve,—
    Demon, sprite, and elve,
The merchant, lawyer, and leach,—
    Each, each, each.
The bishop who will not preach,
The doctor who scorns to teach,
    The well-fed sinecure;
And all, who perforce endure
    Hunger and thirst and cold,
    And more than can be told,—
All for that precious thing called gold!

II.

In the morning's first bloom,
  They gather around

As if summoned by doom,
To dig the ground
Of this ancient tree!
And they cease not their labor when midnight
is o'er,
And, full to repletion, they cry, "Give us
more;"
And, when shadows flee,
Still bound by its fetters heavy and sore
To its slavery,
Its knavery!

III.

All night, in dreams,
By auriferous streams,
Their visions are haunted.
The ocean old,
Is molten gold,
On which, through heat or winter's cold,
They venture, nothing daunted.

Golden the stars that shine at night,
Golden the floods of morning light;
Even guilt clutches ingots of gold and ex-
pires,
And the shorn priest with gold feeds his smoul-
dering fires.

IV.

The pen of the poet is touched by its power,
When basely he panders for Dives's vile dower;
And the voice of the eloquent often is mute,
Struck dumb by the touch of this poisonous
fruit.

V.

It nerves the assassin to strike down his
prey,
And tempts the foul Judas his Lord to be-
tray,—

Disposes both kingdoms and thrones by its lust,
And tramples down freedom and truth in the dust.
It builds its proud temples on lands drenched with gore,
Till blood stains its altars, its walls, and its floor,
And "beam answers beam," as the worshippers stand,
"There is blood unappeased here,—blood on each hand."

PART SIXTH.

I.

Come thou, O breath of Spring,
  Gently thy breezes blow;
Quick all thy influence bring,—
  Thy arching bow!
Scatter thy dower of bliss,
Opening each swelling bud with thy sweet vernal
  kiss.
  Day after day
Still adding flower to flower,
  Hour after hour,
  For aye,
Till, one by one,
New fruits shall ripen 'neath the ascending sun.

What if they fall?
Red-ripe they sure must be;
Nor will we deem that all
Should cling to thee,
O noble tree!
The fruit must have its harvest-festival,
Its buds, its blossoming,
Its gathering.

II.

To its branches we hold,
And we shrink from the mould
'Neath the brave Igdrasil;
But the tendrils are frail,
Storm-riven by the hail
Which beats on them still.

III.

Though severed and tossed,
Though fallen, not lost;

Rich the soil they have found,
In the quiet church-ground,
To which we are bound.

IV.

Mighty harvests are there,
Garnered closely with care;
Angel reapers will come
To gather them home.

V.

Be silent, O heart!
Let the lovely depart:
With their kindred they sleep,
How sweetly! how deep!

VI.

But the morn will awake,
And the glad earth will shake

With a rapturous song,
Which the heavens will prolong.

VII.

"O Death, where's thy sting?"
The ransomed will sing;
"O Death, yield thy trust,"
Will be heard by the dust;
For the Victor is nigh,
Who will gather his jewels to set in the sky.

VIII.

But come not, O Death, when the bud and the flower
In the warm breath of Spring are displaying their power,
And the dew and the sunshine are beaming so bright,
And the heart is so trusting, so joyous and light.

Let the summer-time ripen the promise of
spring,
And the birds all their carols of music shall
sing;
Let the flowers in rich coronals round us now
wreathe,
And their fragrance upon us in affluence breathe.

And if Autumn shall come with its russet of
brown,
Weaving over the fruit its rich velvet of down,
And the clusters are hanging so temptingly
sweet,
Stir not the dry leaves with thy unbidden feet!

But if Winter shall blow with its winds cold and
drear,
And the ripe corn is ready, its leaves dry and
sear,
Then come thou, O Death! and we'll yield thee
thy own,
And silence each murmur and stifle each groan.

But, with delicate skill and with daintiest care,
Death comes to the beautiful, lovely, and fair;
And, scorning the aged, the worthless, the vain,
Most partial, he chooses the goldenest grain.

He waits not the hour when the full bloom shall pour,
Breathing out on the air all its fulness and store,
But with stealth eats the life from the soft bursting shoot,
And destroys all the promise,—the earnest of fruit.

The eye that he quenches, he kindles with fires,
And the tints he despoils, with new beauty inspires;
And the mind that he prostrates, he seeks to refine,
And the heart that he crushes, he first makes divine.

But think not, O Death, that thy sceptre shall
claim
The reward that thou seekest of honor and
fame:
The bud yet will blossom, its earnest is sure,
And the fruit gathered early in heaven shall
mature.

IX.

Wave on, noble tree,
In the clear light shining;
Fond memories for me
Thy rich buds are entwining.
The clambering vines, and their rich, fragrant
flowers,
With the primrose and hyacinths hid in thy
bowers,
Recall to my heart many seasons of glad-
ness,
Seasons of hope, and seasons of sadness.

Bright eyes look out, now haunting me ever,
Faces once bright, pale now forever,
Smiles shining sweetly as the light on you
beaming,
Dark raven locks in the fresh breezes streaming.

Forms gay and graceful as crests of the billow,
On which the lone sea-bird has fashioned his
pillow;
Glad ringing voices as the lark upward spring-
ing
When the heavens are cheered with the notes
it is singing.

I look now and wonder, in dreams fond and
fleeting,
As the scenes of the past from my eyes are
retreating,
Till I wake, and the visions are lost to my
sight
And the fantasies fade in the glare of the
light.

The vision still lingers, and I see now to-day
The loved and the beautiful, long passed away;
They come, as if summoned away from yon clime,
To meet and to greet me at eve's trysting-time.

As the shades gather round me, they silently
come
And beckon me on to their own blessed home;
And among them a matron-form anxious I see,
With a babe now asleep on her low bended
knee.

And I know, by that voice which now floats on
the air,
And those locks thin and scattered, so white
and so fair,
That a fond mother's eye is fixed on me still,
As of old in the shade of the bright Igdrasil.

Groups of boys and of maidens, full of gladness
are seen,
Still trooping along on the old village green;

And the shout and the dance, and the laugh and
the song,
With the wild wassail mirth, bear my spirits
along,—

Seen dimly, for now are my eyes blind with
tears,
As I watch the slow tread which in fancy
appears,
When pale forms, one by one, fade away into
night,
Till the turf covers all from my grief-burdened
sight,—

The maiden that blushed at the sound of her
name,
The boy that was frenzied and maddened by
fame,
The poor that were crushed by the proud and
the gay,
And the rich that had passed as the flowers
away.

The wrecked and the ruined, the wretched, the
lost,
By lust and by envy, by jealousy tossed,
By love and by hatred alike borne away,
To mingle their dust in the mouldering clay.

PART SEVENTH.

I.

The eye of love, far-seeing,
  Sees into things deep hid,
Catches the odors fleeing,
  The light within the lid.

Lips trembling with emotion,
  Or turned away in fear,
Reveal the pent-up ocean,
  The storm within the mere.

The signs which others see not,
  Love sees, and he can tell:
The blushes fade, but flee not,
  Which he interprets well.

The faltering words that tremble
  Upon the tell-tale tongue,
Though art and skill dissemble,
  Are like a song that's sung

When all alone and musing,
  And HE is at the door,
And his name is interfusing
  With the notes that from her pour;

Till by a rap awaking,
  As gentle as a sprite,
Her nerves at once are shaking
  With a most delicious fright.

She knows the sound, the measure,
  The distance, of his feet;
But love hath its own pleasure,
  The scorner of deceit.

So he comes and touches lightly
  Her soft and trembling hand,

And his brow to her how sightly,
His mien how noble, grand!

He speaks to her about her pets,
The canaries in the cage,
The sparkling of the silvery jets,—
Some jest or persiflage.

A blush spreads o'er her modest face,
A tear is in her eye;
She hides it with a gentle grace,
And breathes a half-born sigh.

II.

"Mary, the day is very fine:
The spring has surely come:
The leaves are on the eglantine;
I hear the wild bees hum."

"Last night I sat upon the sill,
Just near the oriel,"

Said she: "the air was calm and still;
It held me like a spell.

"The swallow clove the yielding air,
The lilac showed its bloom:
This rose, then steeped in dew, how fair!
Its breath was all perfume."

If you had heard her voice of love
And seen her artless look,
Your soul would with the music move,
As moves the running brook.

But I was silent, and my tongue
Refused to answer then,
As if an angel-voice had sung
Within a hidden glen;

When suddenly I chanced to spy,
Close in a secret nook,
A little distance from her eye,
An old, familiar book.

And as I raised it with my hand,
  I think, without her leave,
I read, she gazing on the stand,
  "My own, my Genevieve!"

A dainty pencil-mark it bore:
  She heard me praise it well
When last I stood within the door
  Of the old domicil.

And strange it seemed to me that now
  It opened at this place;
And, looking on her shining brow,
  I saw her blushing face,

And thought I saw her turn away
  And look towards the sky,—
The way her thoughts had gone astray
  Upon an anxious sigh.

III.

"Mary, 'tis now one year, I think,
Since first upon the green,
Just as the day began to sink,
We met: none else were seen.

"A violet in your hand, still wet,
A rose-bud in your breast,
A smile upon your eye of jet:—
I need not tell the rest.

"We walked along the lonely way
That winds the distant beach,
And heard the rippling waters play,
And gentle words from each.

"Since then we've met, and hour by hour,
The last the sweetest, best,
As evening shows her mightiest power
With Hesper on her breast."

IV.

She silent sat, and mused the while
  Upon the words I said:
A tear was playing with a smile,
  As she meekly bowed her head.

"Had I," said he, "the power to tell
  What now is in my heart!
But your presence holds me with a spell,
  That bids all words depart.

"Had I the power to win and hold
  A love so deep, so high,
The gift would make me strong and bold
  As an eagle in the sky.

V.

"Love reasons not; it only feels:
  Its language is a look:

The sigh that breathes, the tear that steals,—
  These are its written book.

"And blurred all o'er is mine, I know,
  With these mysterious lines;
But hieroglyphs no meaning show
  Till knowledge on them shines.

"And love's the deepest, widest lore
  That dwells within the soul:
It stands outside the open door,
  And comprehends the whole.

"The heavens are all her own when she
  But casts her eye above;
For her dwelling is infinity,
  The home of perfect love.

VI.

"Oh, strange it seems to me that I
  Had never seen before

The wealth of love that's in the eye,
The beams which from it pour.

"No other voice but thine can shed
Such rapture on my heart;
No other captive e'er was led
To such a queenly mart.

"And yet the price at which I sell
My pure and peerless love
Is that you bring a gift as well
As that which mine shall prove.

"Let us be even,—I to share
The treasures that you bring;
With these no other can compare:
Take my poor offering!

"Love makes me bold: it hath no shame:
I give you all that's mine;
And what I ask is but to claim
The portion that is thine.

"If Heaven but grant me this request,
This dower of bliss, my own,
I'll wear the jewel on my breast,
A queen upon a throne."

VII.

O love, thou art a sacred thing!
It dwells within the pure:
On all that's good it seems to fling
A light that will endure.

Its own it gives, and, giving, gets
More than it seems to give;
As when the sun in glory sets,
The stars are all alive.

Or when the clouds descend in rain
Upon an April day,
The arching bow the heavens stain
With colors rich and gay.

But let not passion dim its light,
  Or earth-born wishes blend
Their shadows with a thing so bright,
  Its presence to offend.

But, purified by prayer and truth,
  From sin and weakness free,
Preserve the beauty of its youth
  With inward sanctity.

She heard the feeble words I spoke,
  And answered with a sigh;
And, though no answering accents broke,
  I read her moistened eye.

I need not speak the rest; for soon
  The solemn rite was done
Which made our life a day in June
  And changed two hearts to one.

VIII.

"'Tis twice seven years since we were wed,
This evening, Mary dear:
How rapidly the time has fled!
The day seems very near

"Since you and I, with plighted hands,
And words of deep intent,
Kissed the dear silken marriage-bands,
As round our hearts they went.

"We did not know each other then
As since we've learned to know;
Nor can we tell the moment when
Our joys have ceased to flow.

"And not a day has come and gone,
But some new light has shed
Its radiant beauty fresh upon
Your trusting heart and head.

"Not all of pleasure, much of pain,
  Have been our earthly lot;
But time has left on you no stain,
  Nor memory a blot.

"What deep heart-histories linger round
  Our own, our happy home!
The very spot seems hallowed ground,
  From which I ne'er would roam.

"These four old walls within them keep
  How much to fan our love!
The rooms in which our children sleep,
  Through which their footsteps move.

"How many memories crowd this hour,
  Of things long done and said,
The magic of whose mighty power
  We feel, though they have fled!

"A world of feeling and of thought,
  To soothe or to control,

Which from the past this night has brought
  Afresh within my soul."

IX.

Old Juba lay across the hearth,
  His head at Mary's feet;
The cat was full of innocent mirth;
  The baby sleeping sweet.

A sudden flare of mellow light
  The sea-coal shot afar,
And all within the room was bright,
  Nor wanted sun or star.

Minnie—for so they called their pet—
  Had fastened on the cap
Of the little doll, with eyes of jet,
  That slumbered on her lap.

And Henry deep within the lore
  Of Mrs. Barbauld read,

And widely on the downy floor
His well-built city spread.

The clock upon the steeple near
Had struck the hour of nine,
And Mary wept a pearly tear:
It was the twin of mine.

X.

"Just ten years since, this hour," she said,
"And mother passed away:"
The old canary raised its head
And sung a roundelay!

"Here is the spot she used to sit,
And there the old arm-chair:"
Old Juba looked askance to it,
And, rising, sunk down there.

"I thought she would not long remain
When baby sunk to rest:

She felt a cold and shivering pain
As I laid it on her breast."

The cat leaped now upon the knee
Of Elia, as she spoke,
And in the cradle, silently,
The little infant woke.

And Mary pressed it to her breast,
Then kissed it o'er and o'er,
And felt an inward peace and rest
She never felt before.

XI.

The Bible lay upon the stand:
Its leaves were opened wide,
And, holding it within his hand,
Elia these words espied:—

"Their angels always do behold
My Father's face in heaven;"

Mary "of such," said Christ, of old,
Were to his Father given.

Then, bowing meekly at his throne,
They poured a fervent prayer,
That, since their first-born child had gone,
They each might find him there.

Oh, sweet affliction!—doubly sweet
When scattered joys shall lead
The broken-hearted to the feet
Of Christ in times of need!

And through this open door and dark
He deigns to pass within,
Finding the chambers cold and stark
With many a cherished sin;

And with an eye inured to grief,
A heart akin to pain,
He brings the weary soul relief,
And makes it live again.

XII.

Our Lord by suffering learned to feel;
  By want, to furnish bread;
His griefs had taught him how to heal
  The heart with anguish spread.

His home a stranger's here on earth,
  His bed the mountain cold;
A wanderer from his very birth,
  Like a lamb without a fold.

O'erlooking all that pride, or state,
  Or chance to us had given;
To him a man is good or great
  Whose hopes are fixed on heaven.

The poor are rich, the rich are poor,
  Not as we think or see;
But only as they shall endure
  All for eternity!

And therefore sorrow hath a voice
In him that answers well,
And inwardly doth he rejoice
To break its magic spell.

Oh, blessings on his humble head,
Forever good and true,—
The Saviour, who for us has bled,
And rose for me and you!

And blessings on the hand that brings
To sorrow's lowly door
Such costly gifts and offerings
To enrich the suffering poor!

And praises for the words he spoke,
His pity and his love,
And for the bread of life he broke,
And for our home above.

XIII.

Tears fall upon his thirsty heart,
  As rain on meadows shorn;
And griefs and sighs that from us start
  To him at once are borne.

In darkest hours, in storm and hail,
  He comes, as if in need;
And we listen to his piteous tale
  Until our spirits bleed.

He knocks for entrance, cold and chill,
  A beggar at the door,
But coming with his hands to fill
  The coffers of the poor.

XIV.

"Abide with us: the day is spent:
  Share of our poor repast:"

And as he leaves the lowly tent,
  A gift behind he'll cast.

"They know him not:" closed are their eyes:
  A guest with weary feet;
But, ere they from the table rise
  At which he sits for meat,

They look with wonder, and admire
  The words in blessing said,
And their hearts are suddenly on fire,
  While "he is breaking bread."

They know him by his voice of love,
  His look of heavenly grace;
And, while their hearts his words approve,
  He secret leaves the place.

XV.

Stranger, now turn aside thy way,
  And look upon the past;

For life is but a restless day,
  With shadows on it cast.

We guide our pen with trembling hand,
  To lift the partial veil
That hides the bark that nears the strand,
  Borne by the sweeping gale.

By love and sorrow rendered dear,
  Too sacred to reveal!
The records of a smile or tear,
  Which every heart must feel.

And the deepest roots of feeling thread
  Through sorrow's plastic mould,
As the oaks their widest branches spread
  Within the moistened wold.

And only on the turbid stream,
  To its own heaven true,
Will the rich lotus send the beam
  Of its many-colored hue.

XVI.

"Bettie, the storm is raging loud;
The snow-drift fills the air;
The earth is covered with its shroud,
And cheerless everywhere.

"Alas! how many poor there be
Who want for daily bread,
And wearily and heavily
They press a cheerless bed!

"While sheltered from the angry storms,
Close to our cheerful fire,
How many pale and haggard forms
In cold neglect expire!

"Take now your cloak, and wrap it well;
Haste to old Maggie's door:
A night like this, our hearts should swell
With pity for the poor.

"Since Elia died, I've learned to feel
The wants that others know;
And tears from out my heart will steal
At sight of human woe.

"We were so happy, so content,
Blest with each others' love;
But now I know why grief is sent,
And sorrow from above.

"It is to make us one with those
Who share our common lot,
And feel the burden and the woes
Of those who are forgot.

"His voice is pleading with me now:
His heart, it speaks to mine;
And radiant from his saintly brow
The beams of mercy shine.

"Then hasten through the secret lane:
No danger need you fear;

And soon the lonely cot you'll gain,
  And at its door appear."

Love makes us bold: it guards us well:
  It fears no boding ill;
It throws around a charméd spell,
  That holds us at its will.

No evil spirits can assail
  The heart which it enshrines;
Nor can our wishes ever fail
  When love upon them shines.

"I saw poor Maggie leave the town
  And homeward speed at even,
And shivering in her tattered gown,
  By age and service riven.

"A penny loaf I chanced to spy:
  A tear stole down her cheek;
And, as I caught her anxious eye,
  She wished, but could not speak.

"And as around my board to-night,
 Our sweet repast to share,
Her cheerless home was in my sight,—
 Her scanty food and fare.

"And as the howling tempest rose,
 No pleasure could I feel
Until I sought to share the woes
 I am too weak to heal."

Adown the low and rugged steep,
 Through drifting snow and hail,
She sought the lonely, humble keep
 Within the lowly vale.

The room was dark, the walls were bare,
 The windows racked and rent;
And in her manse, with grief and care,
 Maggie in sorrow bent.

Quite old and gray, her wandering eye
 Was sunken deep and low;

Her guest was naked penury,
  Her inmates, pain and woe.

Her arm was leaning on her knee,
  Her shivering limbs acold;
A wreck she seemed upon the lea,
  A lamb without a fold.

"How are you, Maggie?" "Very ill.
  And yet I think that He
Who bade the stormy wind 'be still,'
  Upon the Galilee

"Had more of sorrow, more of pain,
  Than I can ever bear:
He bore our griefs, and would again
  Our heaviest burdens share.

"He hears the ravens when they cry:
  The sparrow in her nest;
And underneath his watchful eye
  He gives the weary rest.

"'Tis well with me: 'tis naught can harm
The objects of his care;
Within no terror, no alarm:
He lives to answer prayer."

"The night is long." "Not very long:
I think of Him all night,
Until I hear the cock's shrill song,
That brings the morning light."

"'Tis very lonely here." "Not so:
How can it be, when he
Deigns with the poor to dwell below
And keep them company?"

"Are you not weary of your life?"
"I am waiting for the day
That ends with me this mortal strife:
I'll go when he shall say."

Bettie returned: she left behind
The gifts her hands had brought,

And felt an inward peace of mind,
  Which came to her unsought.

The winds beat high; the wintry blast
  Impetuous swept the sky;
And, as the howling tempest past,
  Mary returned a sigh.

Her heart was with her boy, away
  Far on the raging sea;
And as each fitful gust would stray,
  It brought fresh agony.

Henry a happy hearth had left,
  In foreign lands to roam;
Shorn of her flock, by all bereft,
  She wept,—a broken home.

For full five years no tidings came,—
  A wanderer from his nest;
But still with hope she fanned the flame
  That burned within her breast.

She waited anxious his return:
  She watched from day to day,
Until upon the smouldering urn
  The last spark died away.

And thus, with many a sigh and groan
  She could not well explain,
Her spirit turned to Him alone
  Who understood her pain.

He knows the language of a tear,
  The meaning of a sigh,
The secret of a hidden fear,—
  Love's deepest mystery.

The weary weight of crushing woes
  Our words cannot express,
Finds One who well their meaning knows,
  To others meaningless.

A sudden rap is at the door:
  "It is the wind, I know:

Fiercely without the surges roar:
 The winds, how rough they blow!"

A heavier knock again is heard;
 Her heart with terror quakes;
And mid the storm she hears a word
 That every fibre shakes.

"It is his voice!" with hope elate
 She ran to clasp her boy,
Returned and waiting now to sate
 A mother's heart with joy.

He makes amends for all her pain,
 For darkness gives her light,
Bringing a harvest now again
 Where all before was blight.

Oh, strange the web which here below
 Around our hearts is spread:
The coarsest texture still will glow
 With many a golden thread!

And sweet reliefs will come at last,
  When least we think them nigh;
As when storm-racked, the tempest past
  Reveals a radiant sky.

EPODE.

FUNEREAL FLOWERS.

I love so well
In the shade to dwell,
And talk to the flowers
In their sunny bowers.

I find them here,
I find them there;
And everywhere
To me they are dear;—

Dear to my eye
Wherever they lie,—
By the side of the pool,
So fresh and cool;

In the garden-plot
By the little cot;
In the secret dingle
Or pebbly shingle;

Under the tree,
Or by the sea;
Through the waving corn,
Or the meadows, shorn.

And 'tis all the same,
Whatever their name.
On the clambering vine,
Where like gems they shine,
In the velvety grass,
Through which may pass
The warm south wind,
Leaving behind
Odorous sweets
From distant retreats;
Or in fields of clover,
Where the rich-laden rover,—

The honey-bee,
So busy and free,
Gathers his own
From the flowers unmown.

But I cannot say
That I like to see,
What I saw to-day
In the hands of sleeping infancy;
Fresh flowers
From the bowers,
Laid on his breast,—
In his hands at rest!
Laid near his cheek,
So pale and meek!
Laid at his feet,
Which were once so fleet!
That these should lie
So near the eye,
Forever hid
From the sight of that lid!

So near the lip
That cannot sip
Their nectared sweet;
Is it meet, is it meet?
I cannot choose to see them now,
As I gaze on that brow,—
On that golden hair,
On those cheeks so fair!
On his hands in prayer,
Folded with care!

PART EIGHTH.

I.

God, who now holds within his hand
  Famine and plague and fire,
To drive the wicked from the land
  Or blast them with his ire,—

Dread agents, waiting on his will,
  Quick to obey his word,
Ready his summons to fulfil
  What time they may be heard,—

Still holds them back,—in love restrains,
  Though hungry for their prey;
And mercy over justice reigns
  Throughout the livelong day.

II.

This one by passion in his youth,
  Unthinking, rashly falls;
Old age, experience, and its truth
  May save him from its thralls.

And this, a rebel in his health,
  In all his thoughts impure:
Perhaps a worm, by hidden stealth,
  His folly hence will cure.

Old age is callous, hard to reach;
  Resistance is its law;
An ice-bound, rude, and blasted beach,
  No sun or rain may thaw.

"I'll send," says God, "the winds to blast
  The snow-drifts chill and bleak;
And in some storm-riven cliff I'll cast
  A word that love shall speak.

"And round its spiry peaks I'll weave
A wreath of Alpine rose,
Whose purple belt of threads shall cleave
To everlasting snows.

"And flowering shrubs, and myrtle lace,
In shaded fissures driven,
Will lend a beauty and a grace
To the azure vaults of heaven."

III.

Selfish we are, and hard: alas! we feel
Our petty griefs, and shame and scorn
A brother's,—make our hearts like steel,
Rough-handling those with anguish torn.

"Mine is no grief," says one, "that shares
Its burden with a generous heart,
Dissolving half its stony cares
In tears that from another start.

"Nor do I deem the world can yield
 So much of pity as I need:
Where shall I find another field
 Yielding so rich and ripe a seed?

"As love spontaneous threw along
 The path on which my life has past,
Each day was like a jubilant song:
 It seemed too precious long to last."

Let us not tramp, as swinish churls,
 What to our sense seems vile and rude;
Lest we by folly lose the pearls
 In searching for ignoble food.

IV.

Thorns of ungenerous thoughts will choke the seed
 That fall upon the rich retentive soil,
Which, to our shame, a harvest vile may breed,
 To show our thriftlessness and mock our toil.

As the dim shadows of life's closing day
  Gather around us from the darkened sky,
The flakes of crimson-cloud may send a ray,
  Calling us upward to the realms on high.

Earth fades, suns darken, and the night has
    come,
  And sleep to weary ones its opiate sends,
Till, like the child at shadowy eve, towards
    home
  Along his chosen pathway eager tends.

And as no vistas please, how bright the scene,
  Or varied landscapes tempt the artist's eye,
Of purple cliffs, or summer's freshened green,
  That look not out upon infinity;—

But only those that amplify and reach,
  Like wandering sunbeams through the tangled
    woods,
Or waters tossing on the lonely beach,
  Telling of weary seas or mighty floods.

So the fond heart, aweary, turns to seek
  Solace and joy from faith's illumined eye,
Catching each glint that sparkles on the peak
  Of mountain-turrets pointing to the sky.

We are not what we should be: life is spent
  In vain endeavors, and in wishes vain;
We feel that 'tis a treasure to us lent,
  To be kept safely, then restored again.

We sigh for what we know not; and we send
  Our thoughts full freighted to a world
We have not seen; our spirits tend
  Upwards and slow, by counter currents hurled.

In love with all that's beautiful, we seek
  For that which is not here; we weep
In fruitless search, and fain would speak
  With those who the rich treasure keep.

Our very life is but a dawn; its rose
  Deep crimsoned, speaks to us of day;

And when the shadowy tints around us close,
The stars their teeming glory do display.

There is nor hope nor joy to man, unless
We look to Him who for us bore
The Cross, heavy as guilt, and lives to bless
Beyond our thoughts, above earth's stormy shore.

Our nature he hath carried to the Throne;
Shrined are the souls he bought, in him;
Through his great triumphs we have found and won
Mansions above the burning seraphim.

THE CONCLUSION.

LIFE AND IMMORTALITY.

I.

How the heavens above,
In pity and love,
On this tree shed their beams!
Every leaf, every flower,
Feels their glory and power,
And with fresh beauty teems.
And the stars rhythmic march
O'er the blue pavéd arch,
Displaying their armor so bright,
As onward they go,
Moving silent and slow,
Raining on us their nebular light.

II.

In the quiet of midnight, at eve, and at morn,
Step by step, their bright banners above us are
borne;
Flaming Mars, red as blood, the stern angel of
war,
And Jupiter, throned in his bright regal car,

And Orion and Venus, now burst on our sight,
Like jewels that hang on the brow of the
night;
And Saturn, whose rings, in their far-reaching
bound,
Seems the type of eternity, mitred and crowned.

And the influence breathing and wafted from
thence,
Regales the faint spirit and bathes every sense;
Of all sorrow and sadness the heart it beguiles,
Like the odor that's borne from Hesperian isles.

Proud boasters! look forth on those clear-written
lines:
Each star is a word, as it brilliantly shines:
The heavens a volume, how deep and profound!
And they speak to our hearts in their limitless
bound.

III.

We may watch the seed
Till from darkness freed,
And the plant has arisen
From out its prison;
And through every stage,
From youth to age,
The germ which unfolds itself to man
Our reason may compass, our senses scan.

But what eye can explore
That limitless shore,
What foot has e'er trod
That unbidden sod,

That divides between matter unconscious and
rude
And those germs in which life bears her numberless brood?

'Tis a sea uncrossed,
In which reason is lost,
In its gulfs and sounds,
Without measure or bounds:
Within, no venturous ship can stir,—
Mid its floes no Arctic mariner.

'Neath its wildering star,
Dimly seen afar,
In the uttermost pole,
Is its ice-bound mole,
And the wrecks of many a keel and spar.
Beyond its walls,
And its dangerous thralls,
No headland lea,
No OPEN SEA!

No city of refuge, to which we may flee
In life's deepest, darkest extremity,
Save in HIM who has crossed
The invisible line,
And was not lost
In the frozen brine,
But has shown us the way
To a world unseen,
Where the bright waters play,
And the fields are green,
And has added the wealth of a thousand spheres,
And a world unmeasured by circling years.

IV.

O life, what a mystery thou art!
What floods in that mighty heart,
Pulsing ever above and around,
In the earth, and the air, and the seas profound!

Its awful beat,
Its unmeasured feet,
Its sounds sublime
Is a musical chime.
Its harmony
Over earth and sky,
The cycles vast of Eternity.

THE END.

STEREOTYPED BY L. JOHNSON & CO.
PHILADELPHIA.

www.ingramcontent.com/pod-product-compliance
Lightning Source LLC
LaVergne TN
LVHW021358110826
845150LV00007B/1699

* 9 7 8 1 4 2 5 5 1 3 8 6 3 *